LET'S DANCE

HiP HOP

Aaron Carr

www.av2books.com

LET'S READ
AV²
BY WEIGL™
ADDED VALUE • AUDIO VISUAL

Go to **www.av2books.com**, and enter this book's unique code.

BOOK CODE

F399904

AV² by Weigl brings you media enhanced books that support active learning.

AV² provides enriched content that supplements and complements this book. Weigl's AV² books strive to create inspired learning and engage young minds in a total learning experience.

Your AV² Media Enhanced books come alive with...

Audio
Listen to sections of the book read aloud.

Video
Watch informative video clips.

Embedded Weblinks
Gain additional information for research.

Try This!
Complete activities and hands-on experiments.

Key Words
Study vocabulary, and complete a matching word activity.

Quizzes
Test your knowledge.

Slide Show
View images and captions, and prepare a presentation.

... and much, much more!

Published by AV² by Weigl
350 5th Avenue, 59th Floor
New York, NY 10118

Website: www.av2books.com   www.weigl.com

Library of Congress Control Number: 2013941098
ISBN 978-1-48961-753-8 (hardcover)
ISBN 978-1-48961-754-5 (softcover)

Printed in the United States of America in North Mankato, Minnesota
1 2 3 4 5 6 7 8 9 0   17 16 15 14 13

052013
WEP220513

Project Coordinator: Jason McClure   Designer: Mandy Christiansen

Weigl acknowledges Getty Images as the primary image supplier for this title.

LET'S DANCE

HiP HOP

CONTENTS

I love hip hop dancing.
I am going to dance today.

4

Hip Hop Style

Hip hop dancers all have their own style.

I get dressed for my hip hop class. I wear pants and a T-shirt.

Hip Hop Clothes

Hip hop dancers often wear baggy clothes.

I wear sneakers when I dance hip hop. Sneakers help keep me from slipping.

Fancy Feet

Some dancers wear special dance sneakers.

I go to the dance studio for my hip hop class. I meet my friends at the studio.

Some hip hop dancers like to dance outside.

I warm up before my class. Stretching helps me get ready to dance.

Stretch it Out

Dancers stretch to become more flexible.

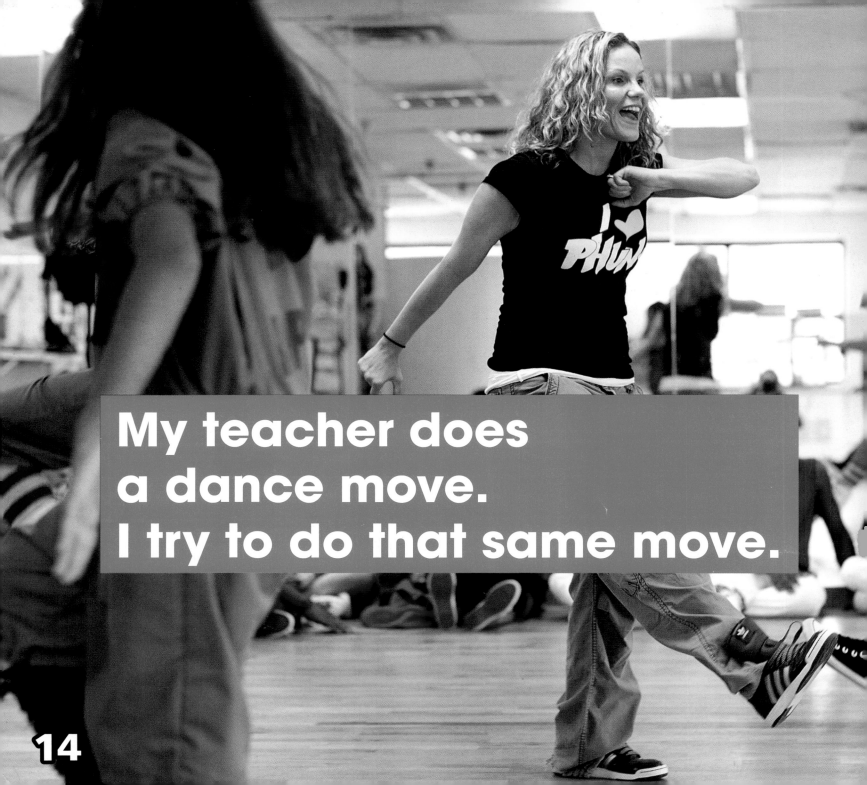

My teacher does
a dance move.
I try to do that same move.

14

Hip Hop Moves

Older dancers
do much harder
dance moves.

I do each move over and over again.
I try to do each one just like my teacher.

Dancers must practice moving to music.

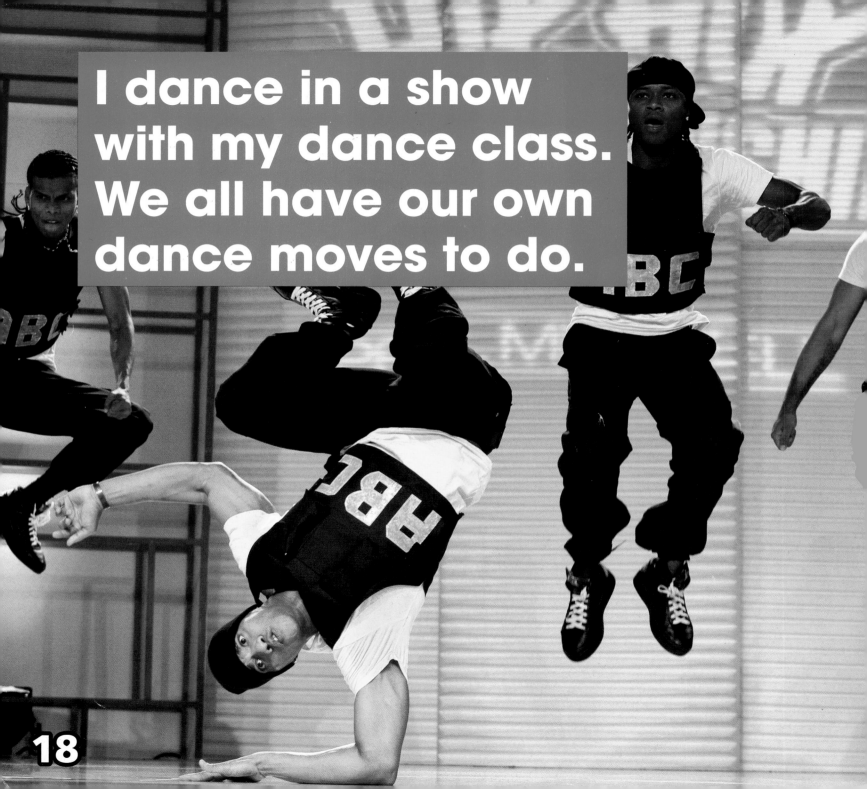

I dance in a show with my dance class. We all have our own dance moves to do.

Hip Hop Crews

Groups of hip hop dancers are called crews.

Hip hop dancing keeps me active and healthy. I love hip hop dancing.

HIP HOP FACTS

These pages provide more detail about the interesting facts found in the book. They are intended to be used by adults as a learning support to help young readers round out their knowledge of each style of dance featured in the *Let's Dance* series.

Pages 4–5

Getting Ready Hip hop is one of the most popular styles of dance today. It began as a freestyle street dance that grew out of the break dancing styles of the 1970s and 1980s. Hip hop dance is closely related to hip hop culture, including hip hop music and graffiti. Over time, hip hop moves were mixed with traditional jazz dance styles. This helped hip hop become more widely known and practiced.

Pages 6–7

What I Wear Most dance schools do not have a strict dress code for hip hop classes, though many schools do not allow dancers to wear shorts. Most hip hop dancers wear loose-fitting clothes. These clothes are comfortable and allow dancers a wide range of movement. Baggy pants, T-shirts, and track suits are common hip hop clothes.

Pages 8–9

What I Need Hip hop dancers usually wear sneakers when dancing. In addition to being a key part of hip hop culture, sneakers offer comfort, support for the feet and ankles, and good traction. Some hip hop dancers wear special dance sneakers. These shoes are split-soled, which gives the dancers greater flexibility in their feet.

Pages 10–11

Where I Dance Dance studios are usually large, open rooms that give dancers plenty of space to move around. They typically have flexible, sprung floors. Sprung floors lessen the impact dancers feel on their ankles and knees when performing jumps and other high-impact dance moves. At least one studio wall is covered with mirrors. This lets dancers check their form.

Warming Up Dancers should stretch before and after every dance class or performance. Injuries can result if a dancer does not stretch well. Hip hop dancers stretch their arms, legs, and torsos regularly. When stretching in the studio, they may use a barre to help them. A barre is a horizontal rail that is often attached to one wall of the dance studio.

Learning the Moves Dance classes may have more than one teacher. The teachers demonstrate the proper forms of the dance. Students watch the teachers perform a move. Then, the teachers help the students repeat the move. In hip hop, there are many dance steps to learn. Beginners start with the most basic steps and slowly work their way up to more challenging moves.

Practicing Regular practice is necessary to learn hip hop dancing. Even simple moves can take hours to learn. As dancers gain experience, the moves they learn become more challenging. The amount of practice they must do increases. Beginning dancers usually have one dance class each week. Experienced dancers practice two times or more each week.

Show Time Each dance studio usually holds two recitals a year. There is often one at Christmas and one in spring or summer. At a recital, students perform a set of dance positions and moves called a routine. Often wearing special costumes, dancers perform their routine to music. Friends and family watch the recital and support the dancers. Wishing a dancer good luck before a show is considered to be bad luck. Instead, people usually say, "break a leg."

Staying Healthy Hip hop dancing, like any kind of physical activity, is great for a person's health. Dancers develop physical fitness, flexibility, and good posture. It is important to eat healthy foods in order to get the greatest benefit from dance classes. Fruits, vegetables, and grains give the body the energy it needs so that it can perform its best.

KEY WORDS

Research has shown that as much as 65 percent of all written material published in English is made up of 300 words. These 300 words cannot be taught using pictures or learned by sounding them out. They must be recognized by sight. This book contains 51 common sight words to help young readers improve their reading fluency and comprehension. This book also teaches young readers several important content words. These words are paired with pictures to aid in learning and improve understanding.

Page	Sight Words First Appearance	Page	Content Words First Appearance
4	am, I, to	4	hip hop dancing
5	all, have, own, their	5	dancers, style
6	a, and, for, get, my	6	class, pants, T-shirt
7	often	7	clothes
8	from, help, keep, me, when	8	sneakers
9	feet, some	10	friends, studio
10	at, go, the	11	fact
11	like	14	teacher
12	before, up	17	music
13	it, more, out	19	crews
14	do, does, move, same, that, try		
15	much		
16	again, each, just, one, over		
17	must, work		
18	in, our, show, we, with		
19	are, groups, of